Devil's Curse Water

S Rob

ISBN:1537026305
ISBN-13:9781537026305

DEDICATION

I dedicate this book to you the reader for without you a book would
not truly be a book.

CONTENTS

ACKNOWLEDGMENTS

To all of those mages of the past and present both male and female who have been killed so that this knowledge exists.

CHAPTER 1

There is one basic assumption that is held by almost all religions people and yet it is so basic an assumption that they do not realise that it exists. The assumption is that there is only holy water and that no other type of magick water exists. But not just is this wrong but just as it has been said that the Devil has all the best tunes he also has the very best magick water. In fact whereas holy water has only the use of being sprinkled around to bring the power of god there and so can be used in exorcisms or for no particular reason other than a blessing, the water of the Devil has many more uses. In fact not just is there water of one devil there are many different types of magick water. But the way this water can be used is not as limited as that of holy water and it can be used to curse many different people, in many ways. It has been assumed for a long time by many people that the water of the Devil to curse a person or an area the water must be sprinkled upon it: this is not true, and here I will show to you the many alternative uses and methods of using this water. Obviously this water can be sprinkled on a person to curse them, but the water can also be sprinkled on an area to cause that particular devil or devils to be summoned to that spot and can therefore he thought of as a way of cursing anyone who happens to be in that area: it could also be thought of as a demonic haunting.

But although items themselves can be cursed by sprinkling the water upon them or even immersing the object within it, the water can also be used for a most systematic and even technically impressive magick, because if it is done the correct way a photo, image or name and date of birth of a person: can also be used to curse the person with the Devil's water. But do not mistake the water here with some fluffy magick that is really new age thought in a different guise, the magick here is very powerful and it is true occult power. But to do this we will not simply be using water but also a small amount of salt. In fact the amount of salt needed for each type of water is just a small pinch, and this is because salt has been known to have the property to absorb magick since ancient times and so the path used here will be that also used to make holy water. I say this in that there are two types of holy water that where the water itself is blessed or made magical and that which is more ancient where the salt takes in the magical properties of the magick and then is put within the water. The salt then dissolves and the water itself becomes magical.

But to do this we will need to summon devils from Hell and so we will be using Leviathan the devil who is himself: or itself: the very gates of Hell. Leviathan was thought in the medieval period by theological scholars to be a large sea monster type creature that lay at the centre of the Earth and so Leviathan's mouth was the gates of Hell and this is why the gates of Hell are still called the Hell mouth, because it is Leviathan's mouth. This means that Leviathan is a gateway being with the power literally to open the gates of Hell and also close it again. In fact Leviathan can open the gates of Hell anywhere and it is through this power that Leviathan enables us to summon other devils. But these devils are not really requested for help although this is what it looks like; they actually are commanded by us. The reason this is so is that human will is the most powerful of forces and when it is coupled with the correct technique it has within it the ability to command even the most powerful of magical beings. This means that the power of these different devils will be placed within the different types of water and with this the power to use this water for magick. But I will now show to you some magick using Leviathan and the devil Carnivale. Carnivale is a devil of the second hierarchy and was a prince of powers: when he was an angel before he fell: and has the power to tempt people to obscenity and shamelessness meaning that this water has the ability to produce erotic effects in other people. You will need a small bowl with a pinch of salt in, some container with some water in it, and something to stir the water and salt together. If you have these you should proceed as follows.

Carnivale devil's water for people to want to act obscenely

(You will need a small bowl with a pinch of salt in and some container with water in and something to stir the contents with)

Leviathan great devil, devil of the first rank, great sea monster of the most ancient of times, your mouth is the very mouth of Hell and so I ask that you open the gateway to Hell right here and now: Leviathan open your mouth Hell's mouth, open the gateway to Hell right here and now. Leviathan open the gateway, open the gates oh great gatekeeper of the damned place, open the gates, open the gateway: Leviathan opens its mouth Hells mouth, the teeth are seen and the gateway to Hell is open for all to see. (Hold the bowl of salt below you while you say the following words) Carnivale great devil of the second rank: powerful Carnivale step through the gates. Carnivale step through the gateway into this world. Carnivale steps through the gates, and is here with me now. Great Carnivale you have the ability to influence others, yours is the power that creates obscenity and shamelessness, and I ask that you place this power within this salt. (While still holding the salt say the word "Carnivale" 108 times and then put down the bowl) The power within this salt I now put into this water, that which is the universal conductor of life. (Put the salt into the water and stir it until it dissolves) This water now has the power of the devil named Carnivale within it and as such is an infernal and damned thing. Carnivale agrees to help and departs through the gates. Leviathan great devil, devil of the first rank, great sea monster of the most ancient of times, your mouth is the very mouth of Hell and so I ask that you shut the gateway to Hell right here and now: Leviathan shut your mouth Hell's mouth; shut closed the gateway to Hell right here and now. Leviathan close the gateway, close the gates oh great gatekeeper of the damned place, close the gates, close the gateway: Leviathan shuts its mouth Hell's mouth, the teeth are no longer seen and the gateway to Hell is closed. So it is and will be.

(The water can now be used by sprinkling it upon a person to curse them; it can be sprinkled on a place to affect those within that place, on an object so that anyone holding the object will be affected by it. It can even be sprinkled on a picture or name with date of birth and can affect them that way)

The water can be bottled and labelled if you wish to use it at some other time.

In order for you to use this water effectively you must try to use it the correct way and so I will now introduce you to the correct way of using the water to affect someone using a picture of them or a piece of paper with their name and date of birth written upon it. However you should know the person or you may find that the targeting aspect of the magick means that it will take longer to work or may simply disperse and not work at all.

Using Carnivale devils water with a picture or paper with name and date of birth upon it

(You should take the Carnivale devils water and have in front of you the picture of your chosen person or the slip of paper with their name and date of birth upon it. Take the water and dab some upon the picture or paper while saying).In the name of Carnivale I curse this person and they will be punished with obscenity and shamelessness and shall live this way always, and in this way they will be damned. So it is and will be.

As you will have seen the magick is not difficult and I imagine because of its ease of making many will simply throw the water away, and in fact if you place it down the drain the water does actually have a destructive affect upon I otherwise all water would be devil's water. But you can bottle it: although you will need a funnel or perhaps placed into old jam jars: but if you do, then label the container exactly so that you know exactly what it is.

CHAPTER 2

The magick within this chapter is the magick of the devil named
Sonneillon, and this devil: one who was an angel who fell: has the
power of hate. This means that Sonneillon can be made to make
people to hate each other, and so bring out the worst of traits in
people. But hate is also self destructive some of the time, and his
power comes in two main forms, it can be used to make someone
hate, or to get others to hate them. Hate can cause people to be hurt,
killed and it is a powerful emotion, and yet most of society does not
know how to use it and so with this in mind here is some magick that
allows you to make Sonneillon devil's water.

Sonneillon devil's water to create hate

(You will need a small bowl with a pinch of salt in and some
container with water in and something to stir the contents with)

Leviathan great devil, devil of the first rank, great sea monster of the
most ancient of times, your mouth is the very mouth of Hell and so I
ask that you open the gateway to Hell right here and now: Leviathan

open your mouth Hell's mouth, open the gateway to Hell right here and now. Leviathan open the gateway, open the gates oh great gatekeeper of the damned place, open the gates, open the gateway: Leviathan opens its mouth Hells mouth, the teeth are seen and the gateway to Hell is open for all to see. (Hold the bowl of salt below you while you say the following words) Sonneillon great devil of the first rank: powerful Sonneillon step through the gates. Sonneillon step through the gateway into this world. Sonneillon steps through the gates, and is here with me now. Great Sonneillon you have the power to create hate and through you people can be caused to hate and so damned, and I ask that you place this power within this salt. (While still holding the salt say the word "Sonneillon" 108 times and then put down the bowl) The power within this salt I now put into this water, that which is the universal conductor of life. (Put the salt into the water and stir it until it dissolves) This water now has the power of the devil named Sonneillon within it and as such is an infernal and damned thing. Sonneillon agrees to help and departs through the gates. Leviathan great devil, devil of the first rank, great sea monster of the most ancient of times, your mouth is the very mouth of Hell and so I ask that you shut the gateway to Hell right here and now: Leviathan shut your mouth Hell's mouth; shut closed the gateway to Hell right here and now. Leviathan close the gateway, close the gates oh great gatekeeper of the damned place, close the gates, close the gateway: Leviathan shuts its mouth Hell's mouth, the teeth are no longer seen and the gateway to Hell is closed. So it is and will be.

(The water can now be used by sprinkling it upon a person to curse them; it can be sprinkled on a place to affect those within that place, on an object so that anyone holding the object will be affected by it. It can even be sprinkled on a picture or name with date of birth and can affect them that way)

The water can be bottled and labelled if you wish to use it at some other time.

The following magick will allow you to use the water already shown to you in this chapter for you to create hate in someone using a picture or even a slip of paper with their name and date of birth upon. But this magick will create hate which will not escape and will simply stay within them: a most destructive force.

Using Sonneillon devil's water to create hate to make someone be damned through hate

(You should take the Sonneillon devils water and have in front of you the picture of your chosen person or slip of paper with their name and date of birth upon it. Take the water and dab some upon the picture or paper while saying).In the name of Sonneillon I curse this person and they will be punished by being made to hate, and shall live with this internally always, and in this way they will be damned. So it is and will be.

I will now teach to you some magick that will allow you to make Sonneillon devil's water that makes other people want to hate someone: this water will have a similar affect upon an area to the last but quite a different effect when used upon an individual, either by sprinkling it upon them, or by using the devil's water upon a picture or drawing or even slip of paper with their name and date of birth on.

Sonneillon devil's water to attract hate

(You will need a small bowl with a pinch of salt in and some container with water in and something to stir the contents with)

Leviathan great devil, devil of the first rank, great sea monster of the most ancient of times, your mouth is the very mouth of Hell and so I ask that you open the gateway to Hell right here and now: Leviathan open your mouth Hell's mouth, open the gateway to Hell right here and now. Leviathan open the gateway, open the gates oh great gatekeeper of the damned place, open the gates, open the gateway: Leviathan opens its mouth Hells mouth, the teeth are seen and the gateway to Hell is open for all to see. (Hold the bowl of salt below you while you say the following words) Sonneillon great devil of the first rank: powerful Sonneillon step through the gates. Sonneillon step through the gateway into this world. Sonneillon steps through the gates, and is here with me now. Great Sonneillon you have the power to attract hate and through you people can be hated and damned and I ask that you place this power to attract hate within this salt. (While still holding the salt say the word "Sonneillon" 108 times and then put down the bowl) The power within this salt I now put into this water, that which is the universal conductor of life. (Put the salt into the water and stir it until it dissolves) This water now has the power of the devil named Sonneillon within it and as such is an infernal and damned thing. Sonneillon agrees to help and departs through the gates. Leviathan great devil, devil of the first rank, great sea monster of the most ancient of times, your mouth is the very mouth of Hell and so I ask that you shut the gateway to Hell right here and now: Leviathan shut your mouth Hell's mouth; shut closed the gateway to Hell right here and now. Leviathan close the gateway, close the gates oh great gatekeeper of the damned place, close the gates, close the gateway: Leviathan shuts its mouth Hell's mouth, the teeth are no longer seen and the gateway to Hell is closed. So it is and will be.

(The water can now be used by sprinkling it upon a person to curse them; it can be sprinkled on a place to affect those within that place, on an object so that anyone holding the object will be affected by it. It can even be sprinkled on a picture or name with date of birth and can affect them that way)

The water can be bottled and labelled if you wish to use it at some other time.

The ritual may seem quite similar but actually the water is quite different because the first Sonneillon devil's water was for it to make hate, the other is to attract hate. So if you sprinkle the water around an area the first will make those within that area hate, and the second will attract hate to those when they are in the area. But when used upon a person it will make people hate them.

Using Sonneillon devil's water to make other people hate someone

(You should take the Sonneillon devils water and have in front of you the picture of your chosen person, or slip of paper with their name and date of birth upon. Take the water and dab some upon the picture or paper while saying).In the name of Sonneillon I curse this person and they will be hated by others and those that hate will be attracted to them always, and shall live with this always, and in this way they will be damned. So it is and will be.

CHAPTER 3

I will now teach you to call upon the devil Gressil and place his power within salt and so into the water this dissolves into. Gressil is a devil and this means he was an angel who fell from grace. In fact Gressil was a prince of thrones: a type of angel: when he was an angel before he fell. But Gressil is of the first rank: if classified using the classification of Sebastien Michaelis which is the one I use because it is the only one that makes sense and mirrors that of angels. Here is how to make the water using Gressil.

Gressil devil's water to create permissiveness

(You will need a small bowl with a pinch of salt in and some container with water in and something to stir the contents with)

Leviathan great devil, devil of the first rank, great sea monster of the most ancient of times, your mouth is the very mouth of Hell and so I ask that you open the gateway to Hell right here and now: Leviathan open your mouth Hell's mouth, open the gateway to Hell right here and now. Leviathan open the gateway, open the gates oh great gatekeeper of the damned place, open the gates, open the gateway: Leviathan opens its mouth Hells mouth, the teeth are seen and the gateway to Hell is open for all to see. (Hold the bowl of salt below you while you say the following words) Gressil great devil of the first rank: powerful Gressil step through the gates. Gressil step through the gateway into this world. Gressil steps through the gates, and is here with me now. Great Gressil you have the power to create sexual permissiveness and through you people can be caused to throw aside sexual purity and share themselves abundantly and so be damned, and I ask that you place this power within this salt. (While still holding the salt say the word "Gressil" 108 times and then put down the bowl) The power within this salt I now put into this water, that which is the universal conductor of life. (Put the salt into the water and stir it until it dissolves) This water now has the power of the devil named Gressil within it and as such is an infernal and damned thing. Gressil agrees to help and departs through the gates. Leviathan great devil, devil of the first rank, great sea monster of the most ancient of times, your mouth is the very mouth of Hell and so I ask that you shut the gateway to Hell right here and now: Leviathan shut your mouth Hell's mouth; shut closed the gateway to Hell right here and now. Leviathan close the gateway, close the gates oh great gatekeeper of the damned place, close the gates, close the gateway: Leviathan shuts its mouth Hell's mouth, the teeth are no longer seen and the gateway to Hell is closed. So it is and will be.

(The water can now be used by sprinkling it upon a person to curse them; it can be sprinkled on a place to affect those within that place, on an object so that anyone holding the object will be affected by it. It can even be sprinkled on a picture or name with date of birth and can affect them that way)

The water can be bottled and labelled if you wish to use it at some other time.

I will next show to you the way of using the water already shown to you in this chapter so that you can make anyone who you wish to sexually permissive; be they nun even this magick will work.

Using Gressil devil's water to make someone sexually permissive

(You should take the Gressil devils water and have in front of you the picture of your chosen person or slip of paper with their name and date of birth upon it. Take the water and dab some upon the picture or paper while saying).In the name of Gressil I curse this person and they will be transformed and made sexually permissive and will forever be a whore, and shall live with this way always, and in this way they will be damned. So it is and will be.

But I will now show to you the way of making Gressil devil's water to attract sexual permissiveness and this is quite different from the last type of Gressil devil's water.

Gressil devil's water to attract sexual permissiveness

(You will need a small bowl with a pinch of salt in and some container with water in and something to stir the contents with)

Leviathan great devil, devil of the first rank, great sea monster of the most ancient of times, your mouth is the very mouth of Hell and so I ask that you open the gateway to Hell right here and now: Leviathan open your mouth Hell's mouth, open the gateway to Hell right here and now. Leviathan open the gateway, open the gates oh great gatekeeper of the damned place, open the gates, open the gateway: Leviathan opens its mouth Hells mouth, the teeth are seen and the gateway to Hell is open for all to see. (Hold the bowl of salt below you while you say the following words) Gressil great devil of the first rank: powerful Gressil step through the gates. Gressil step through the gateway into this world. Gressil steps through the gates, and is here with me now. Great Gressil you have the power to attract sexual permissiveness and through you people will find sexual permissive people will be attracted to them and wish to share themselves abundantly and so be damned, and I ask that you place this power within this salt. (While still holding the salt say the word "Gressil" 108 times and then put down the bowl) The power within this salt I now put into this water, that which is the universal conductor of life. (Put the salt into the water and stir it until it dissolves) This water now has the power of the devil named Gressil within it and as such is an infernal and damned thing. Gressil agrees to help and departs through the gates. Leviathan great devil, devil of the first rank, great sea monster of the most ancient of times, your mouth is the very mouth of Hell and so I ask that you shut the gateway to Hell right here and now: Leviathan shut your mouth Hell's mouth; shut closed the gateway to Hell right here and now. Leviathan close the gateway, close the gates oh great gatekeeper of the damned place, close the gates, close the gateway: Leviathan shuts its mouth Hell's mouth, the teeth are no longer seen and the gateway to Hell is closed. So it is and will be.

(The water can now be used by sprinkling it upon a person to curse them; it can be sprinkled on a place to affect those within that place, on an object so that anyone holding the object will be affected by it. It can even be sprinkled on a picture or name with date of birth and can affect them that way)

The water can be bottled and labelled if you wish to use it at some other time.

If this water to attract sexual permissiveness is used in an area it will attract people who want to be sexually permissiveness. If this is used on an article it will attract sexually permissive people to the article, but if it is used on a person it will attract sexually permissive people to them: it has the same effect when it is used on a picture or slip of paper with a person's name and date of birth on and this is done as follows.

Using Gressil devil's water to attract sexually permissive people

(You should take the Gressil devils water and have in front of you the picture of your chosen person or slip of paper with their name and date of birth upon it. Take the water and dab some upon the picture or paper while saying).In the name of Gressil I curse this person and they will find that sexually permissive people will pursue them always and shall live with this way always, and in this way they will also be damned. So it is and will be.

The magick you have just been taught has the effect of making your chosen person be constantly surrounded by people who want to have sex with them and act in a flirtatious and sexually permissive way. This may sound ideal but to many people this will cause problems, cause long terms relationships to be destroyed, and even pull them into acting in ways that they will later on wish they had not. It is after all magick that pulls your chosen person into being damned in Hell: and for most people this is not their wished for final destination

CHAPTER 4

Verrine is a devil of first rank and this devil has power over impatience and through this Verrine can cause someone to make their own destruction, cause the destruction of others through carelessness: to make this water follow these directions.

Verrine devil's water to create impatience

(You will need a small bowl with a pinch of salt in and some container with water in and something to stir the contents with)

Leviathan great devil, devil of the first rank, great sea monster of the most ancient of times, your mouth is the very mouth of Hell and so I ask that you open the gateway to Hell right here and now: Leviathan open your mouth Hell's mouth, open the gateway to Hell right here and now. Leviathan open the gateway, open the gates oh great gatekeeper of the damned place, open the gates, open the gateway: Leviathan opens its mouth Hells mouth, the teeth are seen and the gateway to Hell is open for all to see. (Hold the bowl of salt below you while you say the following words) Verrine great devil of the first rank: powerful Verrine step through the gates. Verrine step through the gateway into this world. Verrine steps through the gates, and is here with me now. Great Verrine you have the power to create impatience and through this destruction; through you people can be caused to throw aside all else and act before thinking and so become damned, and I ask that you place this power within this salt. (While still holding the salt say the word "Verrine" 108 times and then put down the bowl) The power within this salt I now put into this water, that which is the universal conductor of life. (Put the salt into the water and stir it until it dissolves) This water now has the power of the devil named Verrine within it and as such is an infernal and damned thing. Verrine agrees to help and departs through the gates. Leviathan great devil, devil of the first rank, great sea monster of the most ancient of times, your mouth is the very mouth of Hell and so I ask that you shut the gateway to Hell right here and now: Leviathan shut your mouth Hell's mouth; shut closed the gateway to Hell right here and now. Leviathan close the gateway, close the gates oh great gatekeeper of the damned place, close the gates, close the gateway: Leviathan shuts its mouth Hell's mouth, the teeth are no longer seen and the gateway to Hell is closed. So it is and will be.

(The water can now be used by sprinkling it upon a person to curse them; it can be sprinkled on a place to affect those within that place, on an object so that anyone holding the object will be affected by it. It can even be sprinkled on a picture or name with date of birth and can affect them that way)

The water can be bottled and labelled if you wish to use it at some other time.

The Verrine devil's water can be sprinkled on an area and it will cause those within the area to make mistakes and if sprinkled upon a person it will cause that person to make mistakes but to use this water on a picture of someone or a slip of paper with their name and date of birth perform these directions.

Using Verrine devil's water to make someone impatient

(You should take the Verrine devils water and have in front of you the picture of your chosen person or slip of paper with their name and date of birth upon it. Take the water and dab some upon the picture or paper while saying).In the name of Verrine I curse this person and they will be transformed and made impatient and will always rush to failure, and shall live with this always, and in this way they will be damned. So it is and will be.

The devils water I now show you how to make is to attract impatient people. This will mean that this water will cause people to suffer: but not through their own acts: but through the mistakes of other people and it is made as follows.

Verrine devil's water to attract impatient people

(You will need a small bowl with a pinch of salt in and some container with water in and something to stir the contents with)

Leviathan great devil, devil of the first rank, great sea monster of the most ancient of times, your mouth is the very mouth of Hell and so I ask that you open the gateway to Hell right here and now: Leviathan open your mouth Hell's mouth, open the gateway to Hell right here and now. Leviathan open the gateway, open the gates oh great gatekeeper of the damned place, open the gates, open the gateway: Leviathan opens its mouth Hells mouth, the teeth are seen and the gateway to Hell is open for all to see. (Hold the bowl of salt below you while you say the following words) Verrine great devil of the first rank: powerful Verrine step through the gates. Verrine step through the gateway into this world. Verrine steps through the gates, and is here with me now. Great Verrine you have the power to attract impatience so that impatient people will be attracted and through this destruction will be caused and so become damned, and I ask that you place this power within this salt. (While still holding the salt say the word "Verrine" 108 times and then put down the bowl) The power within this salt I now put into this water, that which is the universal conductor of life. (Put the salt into the water and stir it until it dissolves) This water now has the power of the devil named Verrine within it and as such is an infernal and damned thing. Verrine agrees to help and departs through the gates. Leviathan great devil, devil of the first rank, great sea monster of the most ancient of times, your mouth is the very mouth of Hell and so I ask that you shut the gateway to Hell right here and now: Leviathan shut your mouth Hell's mouth; shut closed the gateway to Hell right here and now. Leviathan close the gateway, close the gates oh great gatekeeper of the damned place, close the gates, close the gateway: Leviathan shuts its mouth Hell's mouth, the teeth are no longer seen and the gateway to Hell is closed. So it is and will be.

(The water can now be used by sprinkling it upon a person to curse them; it can be sprinkled on a place to affect those within that place, on an object so that anyone holding the object will be affected by it. It can even be sprinkled on a picture or name with date of birth and can affect them that way)

The water can be bottled and labelled if you wish to use it at some other time.

If the Verrine devil's water to attract impatient people is used on an area it will attract people who are impatient and likely to make mistakes: it would therefore cause a huge accident if sprinkled at a nuclear power station. If sprinkled on a person it will cause them to be surrounded by these people and ultimately harmed by their mistakes. To use this water upon the picture of a person or a slip of paper with their name and date of birth and so affect them from a distance perform this ritual.

Using Verrine devil's water to attract impatient people

(You should take the Verrine devils water and have in front of you the picture of your chosen person or slip of paper with their name and date of birth upon it. Take the water and dab some upon the picture or paper while saying).In the name of Verrine I curse this person and they will have impatient and careless people attracted to them always and through this destruction and failure will be caused and in this way they too will be damned. So it is and will be.

The magick you have so far learned have shown that sometimes small things such as impatience can create problems and even lure someone to damnation. In fact much of the time the more powerful devils have powers that are less obvious but very powerful. Most of all do use this water when you think it is appropriate. But you can store this water away in a bottle, but you should label the bottle with all relevant details. I know that some people worry what type of bottle they use but this is not fiction and it is not needed and so simply get any empty bottle wash it first and take off the label: put the devils water within: put on a new label with the details of the water and what type it is.

CHAPTER 5

This chapter uses the power of the devil name Astaroth, and through this much can be stopped. The power he has is that of laziness and through him nothing can happen, and all stops except the damnation he causes. He is a devil of the first rank and so very powerful and so he should never be underestimated or the dangers of laziness. To make Astaroth devil's water to create laziness: follow these instructions.

Astaroth devil's water to create laziness

(You will need a small bowl with a pinch of salt in and some container with water in and something to stir the contents with)

Leviathan great devil, devil of the first rank, great sea monster of the most ancient of times, your mouth is the very mouth of Hell and so I ask that you open the gateway to Hell right here and now: Leviathan open your mouth Hell's mouth, open the gateway to Hell right here and now. Leviathan open the gateway, open the gates oh great gatekeeper of the damned place, open the gates, open the gateway:

Leviathan opens its mouth Hells mouth, the teeth are seen and the gateway to Hell is open for all to see. (Hold the bowl of salt below you while you say the following words) Astaroth great devil of the first rank: powerful Astaroth step through the gates. Astaroth step through the gateway into this world. Astaroth steps through the gates, and is here with me now. Great Astaroth you have the power to create laziness and through this destroy all creativity and the fruits of labour; through you people can be caused to do nothing and so become damned, and I ask that you place this power within this salt. (While still holding the salt say the word "Astaroth" 108 times and then put down the bowl) The power within this salt I now put into this water, that which is the universal conductor of life. (Put the salt into the water and stir it until it dissolves) This water now has the power of the devil named Astaroth within it and as such is an infernal and damned thing. Astaroth agrees to help and departs through the gates. Leviathan great devil, devil of the first rank, great sea monster of the most ancient of times, your mouth is the very mouth of Hell and so I ask that you shut the gateway to Hell right here and now: Leviathan shut your mouth Hell's mouth; shut closed the gateway to Hell right here and now. Leviathan close the gateway, close the gates oh great gatekeeper of the damned place, close the gates, close the gateway: Leviathan shuts its mouth Hell's mouth, the teeth are no longer seen and the gateway to Hell is closed. So it is and will be.

(The water can now be used by sprinkling it upon a person to curse them; it can be sprinkled on a place to affect those within that place, on an object so that anyone holding the object will be affected by it.

It can even be sprinkled on a picture or name with date of birth and can affect them that way)

The water can be bottled and labelled if you wish to use it at some other time.

If the Astaroth devil's water is used upon an area all those within that area will be made lazy. But if it is used on a person that person will become so lazy everything in their life will cease. To do this you can sprinkle the water upon them but to use a picture or piece of paper with their details upon perform the next ritual.

Using Astaroth devil's water to make someone lazy

(You should take the Astaroth devils water and have in front of you the picture of your chosen person or slip of paper with their name and date of birth upon it. Take the water and dab some upon the picture or paper while saying).In the name of Astaroth I curse this person and they will be transformed and made lazy and will achieve nothing and shall live with this curse always, and in this way they will be damned. So it is and will be.

The Astaroth devils water that I will now teach you how to make is different from the last because it does not create laziness: it does not make people lazy: it attracts lazy people. But this power is more than enough to cause problems for any cursed person: to make this water perform this ritual.

Astaroth devil's water to attract lazy people

(You will need a small bowl with a pinch of salt in and some container with water in and something to stir the contents with)

Leviathan great devil, devil of the first rank, great sea monster of the most ancient of times, your mouth is the very mouth of Hell and so I ask that you open the gateway to Hell right here and now: Leviathan open your mouth Hell's mouth, open the gateway to Hell right here and now. Leviathan open the gateway, open the gates oh great gatekeeper of the damned place, open the gates, open the gateway: Leviathan opens its mouth Hells mouth, the teeth are seen and the gateway to Hell is open for all to see. (Hold the bowl of salt below you while you say the following words) Astaroth great devil of the first rank: powerful Astaroth step through the gates. Astaroth step through the gateway into this world. Astaroth steps through the gates, and is here with me now. Great Astaroth you have the power to attract laziness and through this attract lazy people and so nothing will be done so become damned, and I ask that you place this power within this salt. (While still holding the salt say the word "Astaroth" 108 times and then put down the bowl) The power within this salt I now put into this water, that which is the universal conductor of life. (Put the salt into the water and stir it until it dissolves) This water now has the power of the devil named Astaroth within it and as such is an infernal and damned thing. Astaroth agrees to help and departs through the gates. Leviathan great devil, devil of the first rank, great sea monster of the most ancient of times, your mouth is the very mouth of Hell and so I ask that you shut the gateway to Hell right here and now: Leviathan shut your mouth Hell's mouth; shut closed the gateway to Hell right here and now. Leviathan close the gateway, close the gates oh great gatekeeper of the damned place, close the gates, close the gateway: Leviathan shuts its mouth Hell's mouth, the teeth are no longer seen and the gateway to Hell is closed. So it is and will be.

(The water can now be used by sprinkling it upon a person to curse them; it can be sprinkled on a place to affect those within that place, on an object so that anyone holding the object will be affected by it. It can even be sprinkled on a picture or name with date of birth and can affect them that way)

The water can be bottled and labelled if you wish to use it at some other time.

If the water you have just learnt how to make is used on an area it will populate it with lazy people. But if it is used on a person it will mean that whenever they need someone, that person will be lazy and will not perform the necessary function causing many headaches.

Using Astaroth devil's water to attract lazy people

(You should take the Astaroth devils water and have in front of you the picture of your chosen person or slip of paper with their name and date of birth upon it. Take the water and dab some upon the picture or paper while saying).In the name of Astaroth I curse this person and lazy people will be attracted to and surround them always and so nothing will be achieved and they shall live with this curse always, and in this way they will be damned. So it is and will be.

The power of the devil Astaroth is commanded by you because you are more powerful than he is. Your will is so powerful that when it is used the correct way is can literally move powerful devils to obey your commands and so make the water be empowered by their abilities. This magick will allow you to use that which will prove useful for some right away and for some perhaps later on, but it will prove useful.

CHAPTER 6

Berith is a devil whose power is murder, and the ability to create the wish to kill in others. This means that many murders happen through the influence of Berith, and what he does therefore is the most violent of damnations because he causes the death of the innocent. But if you wish to unleash the power of this dangerous devil by placing it into water for your use then perform this ritual.

Berith devil's water to create the wish to kill

(You will need a small bowl with a pinch of salt in and some container with water in and something to stir the contents with)

Leviathan great devil, devil of the first rank, great sea monster of the most ancient of times, your mouth is the very mouth of Hell and so I ask that you open the gateway to Hell right here and now: Leviathan open your mouth Hell's mouth, open the gateway to Hell right here and now. Leviathan open the gateway, open the gates oh great gatekeeper of the damned place, open the gates, open the gateway: Leviathan opens its mouth Hells mouth, the teeth are seen and the gateway to Hell is open for all to see. (Hold the bowl of salt below you while you say the following words) Berith great devil of the first rank: powerful Berith step through the gates. Berith step through the gateway into this world. Berith steps through the gates, and is here with me now. Great Berith you have the power to create homicide, the wish to kill and through this murder and destruction and so damned, and I ask that you place this power within this salt. (While still holding the salt say the word "Berith" 108 times and then put down the bowl) The power within this salt I now put into this water, that which is the universal conductor of life. (Put the salt into the water and stir it until it dissolves) This water now has the power of the devil named Berith within it and as such is an infernal and damned thing. Berith agrees to help and departs through the gates. Leviathan great devil, devil of the first rank, great sea monster of the most ancient of times, your mouth is the very mouth of Hell and so I ask that you shut the gateway to Hell right here and now: Leviathan shut your mouth Hell's mouth; shut closed the gateway to Hell right here and now. Leviathan close the gateway, close the gates oh great gatekeeper of the damned place, close the gates, close the gateway: Leviathan shuts its mouth Hell's mouth, the teeth are no longer seen and the gateway to Hell is closed. So it is and will be.

(The water can now be used by sprinkling it upon a person to curse them; it can be sprinkled on a place to affect those within that place, on an object so that anyone holding the object will be affected by it. It can even be sprinkled on a picture or name with date of birth and can affect them that way)

The water can be bottled and labelled if you wish to use it at some other time.

The Berith devil's water to create the wish to kill if used in an area: by sprinkling it: will cause people to be killed there. But if used upon a person it will make that person want to commit murder, and although it will damn them to Hell they will in fact always be this way and maybe even regret what they have done.

Using Berith devil's water to make someone kill

(You should take the Berith devils water and have in front of you the picture of your chosen person or slip of paper with their name and date of birth upon it. Take the water and dab some upon the picture or paper while saying).In the name of Berith I curse this person and they will be transformed and made into a killer and shall live with this curse always, and in this way they will be damned. So it is and will be.

The Berith devil's water to attract murderers will do just that, and it will cause these people to be attracted to wherever this water is sprinkled and so it may be best not to store this water and to get rid of any leftover in some remote spot.

Berith devil's water to attract murderers

(You will need a small bowl with a pinch of salt in and some container with water in and something to stir the contents with)

Leviathan great devil, devil of the first rank, great sea monster of the most ancient of times, your mouth is the very mouth of Hell and so I ask that you open the gateway to Hell right here and now: Leviathan open your mouth Hell's mouth, open the gateway to Hell right here and now. Leviathan open the gateway, open the gates oh great gatekeeper of the damned place, open the gates, open the gateway: Leviathan opens its mouth Hells mouth, the teeth are seen and the gateway to Hell is open for all to see. (Hold the bowl of salt below you while you say the following words) Berith great devil of the first rank: powerful Berith step through the gates. Berith step through the gateway into this world. Berith steps through the gates, and is here with me now. Great Berith you have the power to attract homicide and through this you will attract killers those that wish to murder and destroy others and so they will be damned, and I ask that you place this power within this salt. (While still holding the salt say the word "Berith" 108 times and then put down the bowl) The power within this salt I now put into this water, that which is the universal conductor of life. (Put the salt into the water and stir it until it dissolves) This water now has the power of the devil named Berith within it and as such is an infernal and damned thing. Berith agrees to help and departs through the gates. Leviathan great devil, devil of the first rank, great sea monster of the most ancient of times, your mouth is the very mouth of Hell and so I ask that you shut the gateway to Hell right here and now: Leviathan shut your mouth Hell's mouth; shut closed the gateway to Hell right here and now. Leviathan close the gateway, close the gates oh great gatekeeper of the damned place, close the gates, close the gateway: Leviathan shuts its mouth Hell's mouth, the teeth are no longer seen and the gateway to Hell is closed.

So it is and will be.

(The water can now be used by sprinkling it upon a person to curse them; it can be sprinkled on a place to affect those within that place, on an object so that anyone holding the object will be affected by it. It can even be sprinkled on a picture or name with date of birth and can affect them that way)

The water can be bottled and labelled if you wish to use it at some other time.

The ritual that follows will allow you to be able to use the water upon a picture of the person or piece of paper with their details upon. The water can of course still be sprinkled upon someone. But for those that wish to utilise a picture or some paper to curse your chosen person here is how.

Using Berith devil's water to attract killers

(You should take the Berith devils water and have in front of you the picture of your chosen person or slip of paper with their name and date of birth upon it. Take the water and dab some upon the picture or paper while saying).In the name of Berith I curse this person and killers, and those that wish to kill will be attracted to them always until they are destroyed and in this way they will be damned. So it is and will be.

The power of Berith is an obvious one: he causes murder. But in many ways the more powerful the magick is the more you should be cautious with it. But this magick can be used upon people and you will find that it will help you to deal with especially difficult enemies: because it will cause them to be killed or damned through killing another: they should be at a distance if you wish them to kill another. But the best use of the magick to make people want to kill is perhaps on an area and in this way you can affect a large number of people and this can be used to lower property prices for instance. But the power of Berith is now yours to use.

CHAPTER 7

Beelzebub is the second most powerful devils in Hell: the most powerful is Lucifer. This ritual that follows shows the method to create Beelzebub devil's water so that the second most powerful of devils can create pride. Pride may seem like a small thing and yet through this he can cause more destruction than you can imagine. To make the water: perform this ritual.

Beelzebub devil's water to create pride

(You will need a small bowl with a pinch of salt in and some container with water in and something to stir the contents with)

Leviathan great devil, devil of the first rank, great sea monster of the most ancient of times, your mouth is the very mouth of Hell and so I ask that you open the gateway to Hell right here and now: Leviathan open your mouth Hell's mouth, open the gateway to Hell right here and now. Leviathan open the gateway, open the gates oh great gatekeeper of the damned place, open the gates, open the gateway: Leviathan opens its mouth Hells mouth, the teeth are seen and the gateway to Hell is open for all to see. (Hold the bowl of salt below you while you say the following words) Beelzebub great devil of the first rank: powerful Beelzebub step through the gates. Beelzebub step through the gateway into this world. Beelzebub steps through the gates, and is here with me now. Great Beelzebub you have the power to create pride the sin that damns to the deepest most cursed of places and through this cause damnation and I ask that you place this power within this salt. (While still holding the salt say the word "Beelzebub" 108 times and then put down the bowl) The power within this salt I now put into this water, that which is the universal conductor of life. (Put the salt into the water and stir it until it dissolves) This water now has the power of the devil named Beelzebub within it and as such is an infernal and damned thing. Beelzebub agrees to help and departs through the gates. Leviathan great devil, devil of the first rank, great sea monster of the most ancient of times, your mouth is the very mouth of Hell and so I ask that you shut the gateway to Hell right here and now: Leviathan shut your mouth Hell's mouth; shut closed the gateway to Hell right here and now. Leviathan close the gateway, close the gates oh great gatekeeper of the damned place, close the gates, close the gateway: Leviathan shuts its mouth Hell's mouth, the teeth are no longer seen and the gateway to Hell is closed. So it is and will be.

(The water can now be used by sprinkling it upon a person to curse them; it can be sprinkled on a place to affect those within that place, on an object so that anyone holding the object will be affected by it. It can even be sprinkled on a picture or name with date of birth and can affect them that way)

The water can be bottled and labelled if you wish to use it at some other time.

The Beelzebub devils water to create pride that you have learnt to make if used on an area will simply make it a place of boasting but it will eventually destroy all within that area. But if used on an individual it will always cause damnation and destruction through their pride. This can be done by sprinkling the water upon a person or through sprinkling the water on a picture of that person or a piece of paper with their details on by using the next ritual.

Using Beelzebub devil's water to cause destruction through pride

(You should take the Beelzebub devils water and have in front of you the picture of your chosen person or slip of paper with their name and date of birth upon it. Take the water and dab some upon the picture or paper while saying).In the name of Beelzebub I curse this person and they will be transformed and give too much pride so much that it will cause their downfall and destruction and they shall live with this curse always, and in this way they will be damned. So it is and will be.

The next Beelzebub devil's water is to attract pride from others: so that those with too much pride shall be attracted to them and in this way their damnation will be caused: and not that of the narcissists with too much pride to start with.

Beelzebub devil's water to attract people with too much pride

(You will need a small bowl with a pinch of salt in and some container with water in and something to stir the contents with)

Leviathan great devil, devil of the first rank, great sea monster of the most ancient of times, your mouth is the very mouth of Hell and so I ask that you open the gateway to Hell right here and now: Leviathan open your mouth Hell's mouth, open the gateway to Hell right here and now. Leviathan open the gateway, open the gates oh great gatekeeper of the damned place, open the gates, open the gateway: Leviathan opens its mouth Hells mouth, the teeth are seen and the gateway to Hell is open for all to see. (Hold the bowl of salt below you while you say the following words) Beelzebub great devil of the first rank: powerful Beelzebub step through the gates. Beelzebub step through the gateway into this world. Beelzebub steps through the gates, and is here with me now. Great Beelzebub you have the power to attract pride the sin that damns to the deepest most cursed of places and these people shall be attracted and in this way they shall cause destruction and so damnation and I ask that you place this power within this salt. (While still holding the salt say the word "Beelzebub" 108 times and then put down the bowl) The power within this salt I now put into this water, that which is the universal conductor of life. (Put the salt into the water and stir it until it dissolves) This water now has the power of the devil named Beelzebub within it and as such is an infernal and damned thing. Beelzebub agrees to help and departs through the gates. Leviathan great devil, devil of the first rank, great sea monster of the most ancient of times, your mouth is the very mouth of Hell and so I ask that you shut the gateway to Hell right here and now: Leviathan shut your mouth Hell's mouth; shut closed the gateway to Hell right here and now. Leviathan close the gateway, close the gates oh great gatekeeper of the damned place, close the gates, close the gateway: Leviathan shuts its mouth Hell's mouth, the teeth are no longer seen and the gateway to Hell is closed. So it is and will be.

(The water can now be used by sprinkling it upon a person to curse them; it can be sprinkled on a place to affect those within that place, on an object so that anyone holding the object will be affected by it. It can even be sprinkled on a picture or name with date of birth and can affect them that way)

The water can be bottled and labelled if you wish to use it at some other time.

If the Beelzebub devil's water is used on an area by sprinkling it is will attract those with too much pride: narcissists: and cause problems for anyone else in that area. But if it is used on a person by sprinkling it will cause these narcissists to destroy them. If a picture or piece of paper with the person's name is to be used: and so the person cursed in this way: you should use the ritual that follows.

Using Beelzebub devil's water to attract people with too much pride causing destruction

(You should take the Beelzebub devils water and have in front of you the picture of your chosen person or slip of paper with their name and date of birth upon it. Take the water and dab some upon the picture or paper while saying).In the name of Beelzebub I curse this person, attracted to them shall be those with too much pride and their pride shall destroy them and they shall live with this curse always, and in this way they too will be damned. So it is and will be.

The magick in this chapter is almost the most potent in this book but the most powerful follows in the next chapter because the next chapter draws on the power of Lucifer the King of Hell itself, making the next devil's water the strongest of dark magick.

CHAPTER 8

The ritual that follows is for you to learn how to make Lucifer devil's water: it is the most powerful of all devil's water and so after it is made if you wish to keep it label it correctly and treat it with great care.

Lucifer King of Hell devil's water

(You will need a small bowl with a pinch of salt in and some container with water in and something to stir the contents with)

Leviathan great devil, devil of the first rank, great sea monster of the most ancient of times, your mouth is the very mouth of Hell and so I ask that you open the gateway to Hell right here and now: Leviathan open your mouth Hell's mouth, open the gateway to Hell right here and now. Leviathan open the gateway, open the gates oh great gatekeeper of the damned place, open the gates, open the gateway: Leviathan opens its mouth Hells mouth, the teeth are seen and the gateway to Hell is open for all to see. (Hold the bowl of salt below you while you say the following words) Lucifer King of Hell: the most powerful of devils step through the gates. Lucifer King of Hell step through the gateway into this world. Lucifer steps through the gates, and is here with me now. King Lucifer you have the power over all of Hell and through you the darkest of magick is done and the worst of curses performed and I ask that you place this power within this salt. (While still holding the salt say the word "Lucifer" 108 times and then put down the bowl) The power within this salt I now put into this water, that which is the universal conductor of life. (Put the salt into the water and stir it until it dissolves) This water now has the power of the devil named Lucifer within it and as such is an infernal and damned thing. Lucifer agrees to help and departs through the gates. Leviathan great devil, devil of the first rank, great sea monster of the most ancient of times, your mouth is the very mouth of Hell and so I ask that you shut the gateway to Hell right here and now: Leviathan shut your mouth Hell's mouth; shut closed the gateway to Hell right here and now. Leviathan close the gateway, close the gates oh great gatekeeper of the damned place, close the gates, close the gateway: Leviathan shuts its mouth Hell's mouth, the teeth are no longer seen and the gateway to Hell is closed. So it is and will be.

(The water can now be used by sprinkling it upon a person to curse them; it can be sprinkled on a place to affect those within that place, on an object so that anyone holding the object will be affected by it. It can even be sprinkled on a picture or name with date of birth and can affect them that way)

The water can be bottled and labelled if you wish to use it at some other time.

The water you learned to make last: the Lucifer devils water: can be used by sprinkling it on an area or it can be used by sprinkling it on a person and the result will be damnation and destruction for anyone within the area the water has been sprinkled or the person who it has been sprinkled upon. But to curse someone by sprinkling the water on a picture of the person of even a piece of paper with their name and date of birth upon, perform this ritual.

Using Lucifer King of Hell devil's water for damnation and destruction

(You should take the Lucifer devils water and have in front of you the picture of your chosen person or slip of paper with their name and date of birth upon it. Take the water and dab some upon the picture or paper while saying).In the name of Lucifer I curse this person and they will be transformed and through your power damned and destroyed completely and destruction and they shall live with this curse always, and in this way they will be tortured. So it is and will be.

The method of making this Lucifer devil's water is different from the last because it attracts the damned to it and so you should not keep this water, use it and get rid of it as soon as you can by putting it in some distant far off place.

Lucifer King of Hell devil's water to attract the damned

(You will need a small bowl with a pinch of salt in and some container with water in and something to stir the contents with)

Leviathan great devil, devil of the first rank, great sea monster of the most ancient of times, your mouth is the very mouth of Hell and so I ask that you open the gateway to Hell right here and now: Leviathan open your mouth Hell's mouth, open the gateway to Hell right here and now. Leviathan open the gateway, open the gates oh great gatekeeper of the damned place, open the gates, open the gateway: Leviathan opens its mouth Hells mouth, the teeth are seen and the gateway to Hell is open for all to see. (Hold the bowl of salt below you while you say the following words) Lucifer King of Hell: the most powerful of devils step through the gates. Lucifer King of Hell step through the gateway into this world. Lucifer steps through the gates, and is here with me now. King Lucifer you have the power over all of Hell and I ask that you attract the darkest most damned of devils and I ask that you place this power within this salt. (While still holding the salt say the word "Lucifer" 108 times and then put down the bowl) The power within this salt I now put into this water, that which is the universal conductor of life. (Put the salt into the water and stir it until it dissolves) This water now has the power of the devil named Lucifer within it and as such is an infernal and damned thing. Lucifer agrees to help and departs through the gates. Leviathan great devil, devil of the first rank, great sea monster of the most ancient of times, your mouth is the very mouth of Hell and so I ask that you shut the gateway to Hell right here and now: Leviathan shut your mouth Hell's mouth; shut closed the gateway to Hell right here and now. Leviathan close the gateway, close the gates oh great gatekeeper of the damned place, close the gates, close the gateway: Leviathan shuts its mouth Hell's mouth, the teeth are no longer seen and the gateway to Hell is closed. So it is and will be.

(The water can now be used by sprinkling it upon a person to curse them; it can be sprinkled on a place to affect those within that place, on an object so that anyone holding the object will be affected by it. It can even be sprinkled on a picture or name with date of birth and can affect them that way)

If you take the Lucifer devils water to attract the damned and use it by sprinkling it on some person the darkest of devils will surround them and if you wish to do this remotely by using a picture or piece of paper with their name upon, then use the ritual that follows.

Using Lucifer King of Hell devil's water to attract the damned

(You should take the Lucifer devils water and have in front of you the picture of your chosen person or slip of paper with their name and date of birth upon it. Take the water and dab some upon the picture or paper while saying).In the name of Lucifer I curse this person and the most damned shall be drawn to them and in this way they will be damned and destroyed completely and they shall live with this curse always, and in this way they will be tortured. So it is and will be.

You have now learnt the art of making devil's water of all different kinds. But you have also learnt the subtle art of making use of it. Most people only know how to use it by the sprinkling of water upon a place or person but you know that the power of this water is not limited by the physical: it being magical in nature. Use this water and your enemies and rivals will diminish. Magick such as this has the power to destroy and torture those you want it to. It means that you can bottle Hell and unleash its power with the mere sprinkling and not even upon a real person or object if not desired. This power is yours and you must use it as you see fit: and when you decide the time is right: because this is how this power was always meant to be used.

Made in the USA
Coppell, TX
07 September 2022